I0103601

Duncan McNeill

Life of Rev. Daniel White

with incidents in Scotland and America

Duncan McNeill

Life of Rev. Daniel White
with incidents in Scotland and America

ISBN/EAN: 9783741162541

Manufactured in Europe, USA, Canada, Australia, Japa

Cover: Foto ©Thomas Meinert / pixelio.de

Manufactured and distributed by brebook publishing software
(www.brebook.com)

Duncan McNeill

Life of Rev. Daniel White

OF

REV. DANIEL WHITE;

WITH INCIDENTS IN

SCOTLAND AND AMERICA.

———

BY DUNCAN McNEILL.

———

PUBLISHED BY
EDWARDS, BROUGHTON & CO. :
RALEIGH, N. C.

PREFACE.

Some of the chapters of the life of Rev. DANIEL WHITE were published in the BIBLICAL RECORDER, and met with such a warm reception throughout the State, and were so earnestly called for by many in book form, that the Author and publishers have yielded to the public desire.

Several new chapters are added, and the Author feels sure that the haste with which newspaper articles are usually prepared will excuse any shortcoming in literary merit; but he hopes the subject matter will call forth the attention and claim the interest it so richly deserves. The heroes in the Faith—those who by their lives and labors have been instrumental in "turning many to righteousness"—deserve to shine, as the stars, forever. Greater are they than earth's heroes, fighting for fame, freedom, conquest or gain; for the fight of Christian warriors is against the "powers of darkness," their victories for eternity, and every soul for which they contend, of greater value than a world!

Very worthy, too, are they of noblest emulation and an abiding place in the hearts and homes of the people; for

" Lives of great men all remind us
We can make our lives sublime,
And departing, leave behind us
Footprints on the sands of time ;

> Footprints that perhaps another,
>   Sailing o'er life's solemn main,
> A forlorn and shipwreck'd brother,
>   Seeing, shall take heart again."

Whom shall we hold up to our children as exemplars worthy of their imitation—the Ciceros, Homers, Alexanders and Napoleons, or the men of God, who, through great tribulations, stripes, imprisonments, spipwrecks, and to death, have kept the Faith, and fought on for the glory of God in the salvation of men? Which would they prefer for themselves and children—the empty pomps and vanities, the perishing wealth and distinctions, which this world can give but for a brief season, or the Bible promise and assurance to the finally faithful: "Blessed are they that do His commandments, that they may have right to the tree of life, and may enter in through the gates of the city." "And there shall be no night there; and they need no candle, neither light of the sun; for the Lord God giveth them light: and they shall reign forever and ever?"

Let us, then, teach our children, and seek ourselves, " so to strive that we may win:"

> " For we must strive if we would win;
>   Increase our courage, Lord;
> We'll bear the cross, endure the pain,
>   Supported by thy Word."

AUTHOR.

Montpelier, July, 1879.

LIFE OF REV. DANIEL WHITE.

CHAPTER I.

SCOTCH CHARACTER.

SCOTCHMEN, throughout all the ages, have maintained a character in strict keeping with Scotland, in its rugged, grand, sublime, bold and isolated outline of scenery. Her mountains, lochs and heather-covered hills stand unapproached in their characteristics; so, too, her sons and daughters hold a place in the world's history which no other nation of people has ever filled. No Scotchman is ashamed of his land or race. Wild men of the woods (the translation of Caledonia) they have been; but even in their wildness, they were unconquerable. The armies of the world—the Romans and the hosts of England—found it alike futile to attempt to hold them in subjection. Temporarily they might yield to superior force, but anon the clans would unite, forgetting their petty feuds, and descend like avalanches from their native heights and bury, crush or sweep away all who dared oppose them. Like the wild rush and roar of their mountain torrents, was their fierce and resistless onslaught! History and tradition are freighted with their deeds of almost superhuman valor. Woe to the nation or people who wronged them or dared attempt their subjugation. Superior equipments, strength of numbers, formed but poor barriers in the way of the infuriated Scots, with cross-bows, battle-axes, seythes and broadswords; their "red right arms" knew no abatement till either raised in triumph or unnerved in death.

With them it was

> " Scots who ha' with Wallace bled,
> Scots whom Bruce has often led,
> Welcome to a gory bed,
>   Or to victory !
>
> Now's the day and now's the hour !
> See the front of battle lower !
> See approach proud Edward's power—
>   Chains and slavery !
>
> Who would be a traitor knave ?
> Who so base as be a slave ?
> Who would fill a coward's grave ?
>   Let him turn and flee !
>
> Lay the proud usurpers low;—
> Tyrants fall in every foe !
> Liberty in every blow !
>   Let us do or die !

As in war, so in religion, minstrelsy, poetry, prose, history and the arts. Far back in the dim corridors of the past, echoed the songs of Ossian, "sweet, yet mournful to the soul," and still they linger about the inglesides of earth, telling of Fingal and his deeds. In poetry and prose, Sir Walter Scott, Burns, Campbell, Atoun, loom up and gladden a listening world. In history, Macaulay, McPherson, and others of like power and research, gladden the nations; while among the modern writers and philosophers, her gifted sons occupy the highest positions.

The student of Divinity finds here the ablest expounders of theology. Here have lived and died heroes for the Faith. Here, among her rocky fastnesses have stood forth the ablest divines—the most sturdy reformers and the ablest preachers of the pure Words of Eternal Life. The fear and love of God are not more apparent in any nation of the globe than Scotland to-day. Travellers tell us that Edinburgh, its capital city, is like a church in its sanctity and careful observance of religious rites and duties on the Sabbath day. Cooking is done on the Saturday previous; public conveyances do not lumber through the streets; cars are still; no door for drinking allowed open; men, women and children wend their way pleasantly to the House of God and back to their homes, keeping the Sabbath day holy, and by their demeanor, walk and conversation, rendering Holiness to the Lord. And as in the chief city, so in the towns, villages, hamlets and granges of the realm. From the cradle, the children are taught that the fear of the Lord is the beginning of wisdom; that it endureth forever; and to honor men only for genuine worth, merit and true greatness in themselves, and not for any pomp, pageantry or outer show. Thus reared, it is small wonder that Miss Jane Porter, from the school of nursery tales, should be able to give to the world such books as " William Wallace of Scotland" and " Thaddeus of Warsaw," in which nobility is personified in the characters portrayed; little wonder that her sons, thus nurtured, should go into battle, fearless of numbers, show or equipments, but trusting implicitly in God and the right! Nor is it strange that they would return " with their shields, or upon them." Little wonder, then, that her young men, thus reared, should, when brought to a knowledge of the truth—to genuine repentance for sin and an unshaken trust in the crucified Redeemer—prove true and strong in their entire consecration to the great work of giving the Gospel to the world. They felt the full force of the old Scotch hymn :

1. Behold what witnesses unseen
   Encompass us around ;
   Men, once like us with suffering try'd,
   But now with glory crown'd.
2. Let us, with zeal like theirs inspir'd,
   Begin the Christian race,
   And freed from each encumb'ring weight,
   Their holy footsteps trace.

3. Behold a witness nobler still,
   Who trod affliction's path,
   Jesus, at once the finisher
   And author of our faith.
4. He for the joy before him set,
   So gen'rous was his love,
   Endur'd the cross, despis'd the shame,
   And now he reigns above.

5. If he the scorn of wicked men
   With patience did sustain,
   Becomes it those for whom he dy'd
   To murmur or complain ?
6. Have ye like him to blood, to death,
   The cause of truth maintain'd ?
   And is your heav'nly Father's voice
   Forgotten or disdain'd ?

They walked by Faith and in the light of the Bible, and no power could daunt them; for they had ever before them the example of the blessed Saviour. He left the shining Courts of Heaven and came down to earth, suffered poverty and an ignominious death, that sinners might live; so were they ready to suffer and die, if need be, in His service; ready to "go" at His command to earth's remotest bounds—to bear persecutions or even death for His sake.

As Wallace and Bruce fought; as Walter Scott and Burns wrote; as Stephenson and Watt invented, so preached the heralds of the Cross. No king, potentate or earthly power could restrain, other than by death or a dungeon, such ministers as McArthur, White or Knox. They would preach if their tongues would utter speech.

With the Scotchman, there is a distinct Right and Wrong—the one, he would die to maintain; the other, he would die rather than endure; the one looms up, like his native Ben Nevis, into heaven, as a beacon to guide and to reach; the other sinks down into the uttermost caverns of the deep, as a horror to shun and to obliterate. In peace, the Scotch are as placid and smooth as the bosom of their own Loch Lomond; but in war they are rugged and fierce as their own storm-beaten shores, cliffs and native fastnesses; terrible as an "army with banners." with the plain imprint of "victory or death" on every feature.

Such is Scotch character. And thus they have stood through all time, "wrapped in the solitude of their own originality." Like Scotland, in its isolated grandeur and sublime outline of native scenery, so has its people ever stood, a wonder unto many!

CHAPTER II.

His Boyhood.

Elder Daniel White was born in Cowell, a small place on an arm of the sea, in Scotland. His parents were poor, but very respectable, and followed, from the best information we can get, the business of shepherds, or herding. His father by this business supported his family, and gave them a start in education. He had four children—two sons, of whom Daniel was the youngest, and two daughters. The oldest son was put to the trade of shoemaker, which he had just completed when the father died. Daniel was quite young when this event occurred, and his subsequent education, as well as that of his sisters, devolved upon his mother and elder brother. The shepherd business was discontinued, and his mother and brother procured a seine and small boat, that Daniel, who was expert, active and very bright and intelligent, might help his brother, as opportunity offered, to manage the seine—set it at night and, with the aid of the boat, bring in the fish in the morning. This business proved to be very remunerative. Fish in abundance were taken; and as there was a constant stream of travel by this point between the Highlands and Lowlands of Scotland, the fish, such as they did not need, were readily sold. So his elder brother, with his trade and this added branch of industry, found it easy to support the family in comfort and give a fair education to his brother and sisters.

It was not all smooth sailing with the brothers in their fishery. It was their lot sometimes to meet startling

ADVENTURE

on the sea. To illustrate, we here give an instance:

One morning the brothers repaired to their net, or seine, and every appearance indicated a good haul. Right merrily the boys unloosed their boat from its moorings, and with little observation of the surroundings, shot out to the extreme end of the seine, at some distance in the deep arm of the sea. With light hearts they attached the ends securely to their boat. At this juncture they heard a sudden heavy "splash" in the water, and, looking back, saw, to their horror, between them and the shore, a whale just reaching, and probably offended at the impediment offered by their seine, made a fierce dart forward, sending the affrighted boys for several moments at a fearful speed over the waters. Gilpin's utmost endeavor upon land, in comparison, would have appeared as the pace of a tortoise. The whale at last turned about into the open sea, and the brothers escaped with joy.

THE TRAVEL

between the Highlands and Lowlands of Scotland by their aboard was a means of greatly benefiting young White in his after missionary duties. Here he formed the acquaintance of many families from both sections, who afterwards emigrated to America and were his warm and true friends during his life. He was blessed with a peculiarly attractive disposition ; any one once becoming intimately acquainted with him, were likely ever after-wards to be his true friend. His nature, person and address were all frank and pleasing.

The preaching of McArthur, too, had much to do in breaking down the ancient barriers between clans and demarkations of rank. Before he came, clans mingled but little, rarely intermarried, and different degrees of wealth or blood drew rigid lines of grade or status in society, over which very few, no matter how meritorious or worthy, could pass. His ministry drew all ranks and conditions together, giving people a clearer view of each other, and convincing them that all the good in the world was not confined to the " pent up Utica" of their own particular clan or grade of wealth. He drew immense audiences everywhere he went, and young Daniel White, becoming early converted under his preaching, became himself an earnest minister and faithful co-worker with him. So conspicuous were his virtues, piety and talents, that he won upon the affections and confidence of all, broke over all the ancient barriers of the aristocracy, gained the love of, and married Miss Catherine Campbell, whose parents were land-owners—a matter of importance in Scotland—and of the blood of the renowned Clan Campbell.

Who has not heard the Scotch rallying song :

> " The Campbells are comin', O ho ! O ho !
> The Campbells are comin', O ho ! O ho !
> The Campbells are comin' from bonny Loch Lomond !
> The Campbells are comin', O ho ! O ho !

> The great Argyle, he goes before,
> He makes the guns and cannon roar ;
> With sound of trumpet, fife and drum,
> And banners waving in the sun,
>   The Campbells are comin', O ho ! O ho !"

The mingling of the clans and people, thus brought together by the power of a pure Gospel, earnestly delivered, was in the highest degree salutary to the Scotch there as here.   Elder White found in these "opened avenues" to the hearts of all classes of the people a greater facility of pointing many to the "Lamb of God," than he might otherwise have possessed.   They were made to feel that "Christ was all and in all," and that

> "In Him, they all possessed."

Thus, by the great revival in Scotland (in attendance on which most of the Clans mingled freely together, and forgot their old feuds), many were brought to *feel* as well as sing :

> "Blest be the tie that binds
>   Our hearts in Christian love;
> The fellowship of kindred minds
>   Is like to that above."

On coming to America, therefore, Elder White found members of these Clans, thus happily joined in heart, scattered here and there throughout the broad belt in which he preached.

CHAPTER III.

"THE DESPISED SECT."

ONE of the great evils suffered by the people of England and Scotland, in the times of which we write, was of compelling the people and laymen of the realm to support a ministry imposed upon them by the State. These Royal favorites—often without a semblance of piety, of depraved morals, gamblers, drunkards and libertines—were appointed to "livings" in the kirks throughout the land, and the people were compelled to pay tribute for their sustenance. These "reverends" rarely filled their pulpits; and in the cases of many of them, it would have been better if they did not at all; for they were far more at home when attending a horse-race, a dance, a fair, or a game of chance. These "whited sepulchers," though heartily despised by the people, and a grievous burden upon them, nevertheless lorded it over them with a high hand; and besides living sumptuously upon the scanty and grudgingly given earnings of the oppressed people, yet exercised a censorship over their spiritual affairs, amounting almost, in the subtlety of barbaric cruelty, to the Spanish Inquisition. Woe to the layman or citizen who failed, from any cause, to contribute his exact and full quota to the support of the High Church dignitaries! They were reported, and the strong arm of the law and merciless vengeance visited upon them !

Did they dare to exhibit any want of reverence or man-

ifest any spirit of insubordination to them, then the re-
finements of cruelty were visited upon them in every
way. Such a clergy, elevated, as they had mostly been,
by the police, and over the heads of an unwilling and
even resisting people, assembled to prevent their installa-
tion (for their "living" was secured when "installed,"
however fraudulently that was done), could not have a
fraternal feeling for their flock, or be much concerned for
their spiritual or temporal good. If a true and humble
follower and servant of the meek and lowly Jesus, in his
eagerness to preach the pure Gospel to the almost starv-
ing flock, in some sequestered mountain gorge, lonely
cave or rocky glen, these "clergy" were first to ferret them
out and hound them on to banishment. Relentlessly,
too, they persecuted those who attended the ministrations
of these "true lights" in secret. In vain did the gentle
Christian maiden attempt to steal away, and in solitude
commune alone in earnest prayer with her God; to seek
spiritual strength and guidance, "and by faith, take a
view of brighter scenes in heaven, while here by fierce
tempests driven;" for the prowling feet and prying eyes
of the "clergy," or their satellites, were sure to find them
out.

As zealously as Daniel was watched, lest he should
pray to any save King Darius, were these humble Scotch
Christians subjected to the closest scrutiny, lest they
should seek spiritual consolation from any other source
than the self-imposed high dignitaries of pampered power
over them.

Such is a faint view of the High Church troubles in

Scotland in the boyhood days of Daniel White; nor are
they over-drawn. The writer well remembers hearing
Mrs. White, an eye-witness of these scenes, tell of the
wickedness of the "established ministers" of that time,
and how she saw them placed over an unwilling and resisting flock by the police.

In further verification, the writer may instance the
well-authenticated account of the faithful band of Christians, who, harrassed by persecution, sought out a place,
surrounded on all sides by high mountains, where they
hoped to be able to serve God according to the dictates of
their own consciences. In this deep wooded basin, through
which ran a little rivulet which had its source high up
in the surrounding mountains, and barely found vent
through the close fishures of the rock from the deep
gorge. Sometimes, in the spring and early summer, avalanches of snow and loosened earth dammed the rivulet
above for weeks, and when it broke through its escaping
waters shook the solid earth, descending like a wild cat-
aract, with a sound as of the

"Tramp of thousands upon the hollow wind;"

and on reaching the basin, filled it high up in but a few
moments of time, as the vent from it was not sufficient to
let off the waters but by slow degrees. To prevent a surprise by the waters, and to escape their relentless enemies,
if they should find their hiding place, the worshipers cut
out a secluded winding path to a rocky cave, high up
among the rocks, having but a small opening, and this
overhung with vines and lichens. One Sabbath in early

summer, this little band of devout believers were con-
ducting service in this still and deep asylum. The shepherds and shepherdesses, the miners and the tillers of the
soil were there, from far and near around, attired in their
best and with reverential mien. The aged minister, of
their own choosing, had just risen from prayer and opened
the Bible on the rock pulpit before him, when their soli-
tary guard, left on the heights above to watch for the ap-
proaches of an enemy, suddenly appeared almost out of
breath before them, and reported that he was surprised,
and that the armed troops were even then descending the
only approach to them. A bonnet and the Bible were
left in their hurried rush to their hiding place, high up
in the mountain's side, which they had barely reached
when they heard the blasphemy and horrid threats against
them from the troops who had just arrived. They threat-
ened death by the torture; they swore and used ribald
jests at the bonnet, and cursed the "heretic Bible and its
God." Just then, a mighty thunder, as of falling mountains, was heard; the solid earth shook; a sound as of
many waters was abroad. The knees of the affrighted
troopers smote together, and, looking up, they saw the
white head of the aged minister, in his high cave, as he
exclaimed: "The Lord omnipotent reigneth." In another
moment the fierce foaming waters rolled in, and the
troopers were all drowned !

Such is a brief narration of an actual occurrence in the
stormy past of Scotland. Such were the difficulties in
the way of true piety there. To be a conscientious Bible
Christian, was to be one of a persecuted and "despised

sect." To be called of God to the great work of the ministry entailed with it an utter renunciation of the world,
its vanities, and all hope of preferment among men. They
were henceforth to give themselves to the service of their
Great King, hide themselves in Him, and seek, by faithful service in fear and love to Him, the true "riches,
honor and life" promised to those who, in humility, fear
and love, fought the good fight of faith. For their earthly
king and all the heraldry of power were against them, as
were also the fawning sycophants of pomp and show.
Henceforth they were to consecrate themselves and all
they held dear to Him; bearing reproach, stripes, banishment—or even the stake and flame, if need be—they were
to fight on, and leave results to God. They were to live
by faith; and in the army of the Captain of their salvation, they would enter upon the mighty struggle against
the "powers of darkness," and perish in the encounter, or
over all prevail. What wonder, then, that the true heralds of the Cross should be "mighty in the Scriptures," as
well as of self-sacrificing devotion! No wonder that sinners were alarmed under their preaching and saints made
to rejoice! There was not greater "striving" among the
Greeks and Romans, in their Olympic games, than among
the devout in these stormy times in their efforts to "win"
in the great battle of light against darkness, truth against
error, life against death. The power of the government—
all the powers of the earth—could not swerve them from
their purpose, by God's help, of turning many to righteousness. They had tasted of the joys of sins forgiven and the
sweets of a Saviour's love. Little cared they, therefore, for

the puny power that could but kill the body, but had no power over the soul. Their kinsmen, according to the flesh, their countrymen abroad, and the heathen nations were perishing for the lack of knowledge. God's command was, " Go !"—teach all nations ; desciple them ; feed my sheep. Could they, therefore, be idle? Ah, no! They would buckle on the " whole armor," and put forth every power of mind and body to call sinners to repentance and to faith in God. Such were the purposes actuating the veteran Baptists of Scotland. Of such mould and frame of mind were the true, fearless, humble, devoted and mighty men of God—McArthur, White, and many others—who forsook all for Christ in this trying epoch.

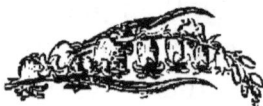

CHAPTER IV.

His Conversion and Baptism.

Scotland is a name very dear to many hearts. It is associated in the mind with daring deeds and deathless heroism. Song, history, romance and tradition, cluster about its rivers, lochs, mountains and braes. Its cities and towns are emblazoned with inspiring memories. It is not only the "land o' cakes," but also of heroes, poets and divines unsurpassed in the world's history.

Here were "Great Hearts," in the truest sense of the term, who, under the relentless hand of persecution, journeyed with their faithful bands of pilgrims and "fought their good fights." In the midst of troublous times Rev. Daniel White was born in Cowell, Scotland, about the year 1784. Under the ministration of the Rev. D. McArthur, an able and zealous man of God, he was brought to a saving knowledge of the truth. This was about the year 1800. There was about this time a great revival in Scotland. But after all, the young converts found a formidable difficulty in obeying their Lord and Master in baptism. The lion in the way was the oppressive laws of Great Britain, which placed a ban upon all forms of faith, belief, or practice not in conformity with the "Church" of England. The young converts chose to obey the great King, in preference to king George the III., in matters of conscientious belief and baptism. The

Rev. Daniel McArthur had to go to a remote part of Eng-
and to be baptized in the true mode, and on his return
chose a beautiful Lake (or Loch as termed in Scotland),
surrounded by butting cliffs and mountains, to perform
the then hazardous duty of baptism to the humble fol-
owers of Christ. Despite secrecy, the news got out, and
on the appointed day, the rocky amphitheatre surrounding the little Loch, was covered with people, rising from
the waters edge, tier above tier, to a great height on the
surrounding cliffs, eagerly watching the impressive and
solemn ordinance. The day was propitious. The birds
sang sweetly, nature was in her fairest robes, and the
bright sun glanced his cheering beams from the rippling
waters to the faces of the happy converts, where might
so plainly be seen " holiness to the Lord," as they went
down into the water and came up out of it,

" Following their Lord and Master
In righteousness below."

At this baptismal scene, which occurred about the year
1800, from the best data we can find, Daniel White, Alex.
McNeill, J. McKellar, Duncan Campbell and Catharine
Campbell, besides a great many others, were baptized.
The names given will sufficiently illustrate the genuine-
ness and power of the good work of grace then expe-
rienced in Scotland. The three first named above soon
after became zealous and devoted ministers of the gospel,
the two latter were brother and sister—the sister was
afterwards the wife of Rev. Daniel White—and thousands

in North and South Carolina can testify to her faithful
ness and zeal in the cause of her Redeemer, while Dun
can Campbell "fought a good fight" for the Master in
Scotland. Rev. John Monroe says of this refreshing
season: "Numbers who were converted in that revival
emigrated to the United States and to Canada. The writer
was personally acquainted with many of them, and can
testify that they were men and women of great moral
worth and devoted piety." After this great awakening
the Baptists, then a persecuted and despised sect, took
courage and preached and exhorted openly, "and they con
tinued steadfastly in the apostles' doctrine and fellowship
and in breaking of bread and in prayer." The enemies
of the Baptists, however, speedily conveyed information
of all this to the Government, and a body of troops were
dispatched to take the minister, Rev. D. McArthur, and
have him before a magistrate where, if found guilty of
preaching the "despised doctrine" against the "Laws
made and provided," to banish him at once to Botany
Bay, the then abode for banned preachers. The soldiers
timed their arrival on the scene to a Sabbath, so as to take
the preacher in the unlawful act, and were followed by a
large concourse of ladies and gentlemen of high degree
as well as of the higher "church." Secure of fun as of the
States' protecting arm, they sported their grandest robes,
with noble hats and bonnets flaunting with ribbons and
plumes. They asked the soldiers to defer the arrest until
they had heard some of the discourse. They came upon
the scene; they saw an earnest minister proclaiming
from a table in the open air the burning "words of truth

and soberness," to a grave and devout assembly; they were conquered, for said an eye witness, before the sermon was ended the soldiers trembled and cried for mercy, the noble ladies were upon their knees and their plumed bonnets and gay robes in the very dust, while their gallant escorts cried, "what shall we do to be saved?" They returned without making the arrest.

A few Sabbaths afterward another body of troops were sent to make the arrest. They came just as the hymn was being given out; they commanded the Rev. D. McArthur to come down as their prisoner. He held the book above their guns, calling upon some one to continue the hymn. An officer trying to snatch the book, his arm fell, as if palsied, to his side. Duncan Campbell and Rev. Daniel White came forward and continued singing, praying, and exhorting while the noble man of God was carried away. No sooner was the brief service concluded than the devout band set about getting up the strongest petition they could to the King, asking his clemency to their beloved McArthur. This Mr. Duncan Campbell took with all haste to London. In the meantime, the Rev. McArthur was hastily tried and condemned, and put on board a vessel to be conveyed to Botany Bay. Mr. D. Campbell, who doubtless went unto the King with feelings akin to those of Queen Esther when she exclaimed, "if I perish I perish," met with favor, and the petition of the devoted christians for the release of McArthur was granted, together with the privilege of intercepting the vessel which was bearing him away, and taking him back to Scotland. This the dauntless Campbell proceeded to do, but found, to his surprise, that the vessel with McArthur on board was in the harbor or dock of London. It had met with a storm and was driven and tossed until compelled to go up the Thames to London. Here Campbell found and released his friend, and with him journeyed back to Scotland. Whether the success of the intrepid Campbell was owing to the importance of the family, (they being land owners in Scotland) or to the waning spirit of religious persecution then observable in England, or to the great trouble and anxiety of the King himself about his soul, which we are informed from history was the case about that time, cannot now be known; but certain it is that man's vile proposals were met by a merciful disposal of the Supreme Ruler.

About this time the Rev. Daniel White, and also McNeill and McKellar, were ordained to the full work of the ministry, and all felt a strong desire to go and preach the gospel to their countrymen in America. In this Mrs. White strongly opposed the will of her husband. To gratify her, though not satisfied in his own mind, he accepted calls and preached earnestly to surrounding churches. Mrs. White often spoke of a sheet of water with its transcendent beauty of surrounding scenery, over which they often passed and re-passed to one of his churches. But we all know how grand the Scottish landscapes, lochs, mountains and rivers are—history and song making them household words in every home. Even these scenes of his fair native land, and the need of the gospel among its people, could not, she said, draw his mind off from going to preach to his people in America. One night she was awakened by his preaching and praying earnestly in his sleep. She saw from his language it was to an American audience. She tried to awaken him but failed. The terrible fear came over her that her opposition to his inclination and God's will had demented him. In an agony of fear she bowed in prayer and besought God to forgive her sin and restore her husband to his right mind, and she would never more oppose his desire to cross the ocean to preach the gospel. When she arose she saw her husband, as if greatly distressed, looking upon her. "Oh," said he, "I thought I was in America and doing God's will in preaching to my people there." And then he went on to describe the church and the people to whom he preached, and we may be permitted here to say (though by so doing we anticipate the regular order of events a little,) that some time afterwards they saw the very people and church he then so vividly described in his dream a reality, and just as he had seen it, in America. How truly,

> "God moves in a mysterious way
> His wonders to perform."

From this time Elder White found his wife ready and willing to accompany him. Arrangements were therefore made for quitting their native land, which, in company with Revs. Alex. McNeill and J. McKellar, they left on the 28th of August, 1807. In our next chapter we will tell of Rev. Daniel White in America, where he left such indellible "footprints on the sands of time," and

from whence he carried his golden sheaves of good works
into eternity.   That "Great Heart" and valiant servant
of God, Rev. D. McArthur, with many faithful co-workers,
remained to till their Master's fields and gather the har-
vests in Scotland.

It cannot be a matter of surprise, therefore, that there
are "Scotch Baptists," but rather that there are not more
of them.

CHAPTER V.

HIS VOYAGE TO AMERICA.

In the times of which we write, and before, there were grave difficulties in confessing Christ before men, or in taking the cross and following Him. We, in these "piping times of peace," can scarcely comprehend the real hardships by which they were environed. When the true christian took the word of God as the man of his counsel, he found Roman Catholicism, with a power almost equal to any of the thrones in Europe, confronting him on the one hand with its enginery of opposition, while on the other hand the favorite "Church" of the King and nation, often little more than a political machine, scarcely recognizing the Bible in its code, was ready to crush all who were not within its pale, or dared to go counter to its teaching. Thus the true believer found himself hemmed in on every side. If he followed Christ, Catholicism hurled its anathemas and direst vengeance upon him, and the "Church of State" stood ready, backed by all the power of the King, Parliament, the army and navy, to persecute, banish, beat with stripes, or even, as in many cases, burn at the stake. He who was called to the ministry, and felt "Woe is me if I preach not the gospel," was confronted by appalling obstacles. The State and the Pope piled Ossa upon Pelion of hindrances in his way on land, while upon sea they were as Charybdis on one hand and Scylla on the other, ready to engulph any herald of the cross who dared to steer be-

tween them. But they did preach. They heard and
obeyed the voice of God, above the rage and clamor of
kings, popes and potentates—and preached, despite all,
to their people, and carried the gospel abroad. What a
sublimity of heroism! What a sweet savor to the nations
when "thrones and crowns shall blend in common dust!"
Though man's puny power did arrest and banish McArthur, yet the faith of the beholders was increased, and
willing heralds ministered in his stead. Though Bunyan
was thrown into prison, yet his bright light from the
damp dungeon still illumines the pathway to heaven!
Though Paul was persecuted, cast into prison and beaten
with stripes, still he "fought the good fight." Though
Stephen was stoned to death, yet his death still preaches!
   May not the christian of the present day, in contemplation of such heroism for Christ, ask—

> "Must I be carried to the skies,
>   On flowery beds of ease,
> While others fought to win the prize,
>   And sailed through bloody seas?"

   The Rev. Daniel White, feeling it to be his duty, under
the guidance of the unerring Spirit, to preach the gospel
in America, left his dear native land, and "all the scenes
he loved so well," for this country. As was shown in a
previous chapter, he embarked on the 28th of August,
1807. Besides his wife, two young ministers, Alex. Mc-
Neill and J. McKellar, took passage with him. The vessel, which was bound for Charleston, S. C., was but a few
days at sea, when they were pursued by a man of war
ship, for the purpose, as was supposed, of forcibly *impress-*

ing any young able-bodied men who might be on board, into the British service as soldiers or marines. This species of kidnapping, so repugnant to every sense of right and justice, was then frequently practiced. Their vessel, however, made all headway, and by skillful seamen and favoring gales, at length entirely distanced their pursuer. Far out in mid ocean they passed a large ship wrecked, and at the mercy of the waves. There were no signs of life on board, and the conclusion was that either all had perished or some passing vessel had taken them off. No other incidents worthy of note occurred while at sea, and they landed at Charleston, S. C., on October 7th, 1807. Here the whole party were kindly received by the Baptists of the city, and so favorably impressed were they with the young ministers, Alex. McNeill and J. McKellar, that they insisted on giving them a thorough course of theological training. All further intelligence that we can gather of these young men is, that they completed the course with great credit and distinction. McNeill, who was said to have been a young man of exceeding promise, soon after died, and McKellar went to preach in Georgia and Alabama.

Elder White took sail from Charleston to Wilmington, to seek out and preach to the Scotch people in North Carolina. Arriving in that city soon after, himself and wife made their way across the country to Lumber bridge, Robeson county, N. C., where he found himself in the heart of a Scotch settlement. Here he preached his first sermon in America, on the first Sabbath of November of the same year. Here, and then, began a great work, the fruits of which the passing years only make more and more apparent. Then, the Scotch people there were sparsely settled, ignorant, rarely hearing preaching of any kind, and hardly ever a Baptist preacher. To this people Elder White preached in Gaelic and English, so that young and old (many of the aged people could scarcely speak or understand English) were fed upon the rich nutriment of the Word of God. Now, this whole people are an intelligent, church-going, God-fearing people. Here his first child, Mary, was born.

From Lumber bridge he went to Richmond county, and there, after a faithful ministry, established the Spring Hill church. This, too, was a Scotch settlement, with characteristics after the similitude of their countrymen described above. Here Elder White's ministry was signally blessed. First, Malcolm McMillan and Archibald Graham, influential heads of families, were converted and added to the church. They were baptized in Jordan's creek.

Some time afterwards there was a great revival in this church. Many happy converts were led down into the clear waters, following their blessed Master in baptism, doubtless feeling in their hearts—

> " Saviour, thy law we love,
>   Thy pure example bless,
>   And, with a firm, unwavering zeal,
>   Would in thy footsteps press.
>
> Not to the fiery pains
>   By which the martys bled ;
>   Not to the scourge, the thorn, the cross,
>   Our favored feet are led.
>
> But, at this peaceful tide,
>   Assembled in thy fear,
>   The homage of obedient hearts
>   We humbly offer here."

Among the seals of Elder White's ministry at this place was Elder John Monroe, who was baptized by him in Lumber river, at a beautiful bluff called Fairley's Ford— a spot yet chosen for happy re-union and pleasant converse in the summer heats.

Rev. J. Monroe is so widely known and revered throughout the State, that we need only say that he has for over forty years stood as a faithful watchman upon Zion's walls, sustaining ably and zealously the cause left in his hands by his father in Christ. The rest of the converts of that great ingathering were baptized in the Shoe Heel creek, near the church.

In this vicinity the other children of Elder White were born : Anna, afterwards married to Duncan McGougan ; Euphemia, afterwards the wife of John Johnson; Rebecca, afterwards wife of Rev. P. C. Conelly; John, who died early; Mary, his eldest daughter, married Charles Livingston. Every daughter had large and interesting families, and themselves, husbands and every member of their families have followed Christ in baptism.

Soon after Elder White settled in Spring Hill neighborhood, he had a call to the Welch Neck church in South Carolina, where, upon his arrival, himself and wife saw, to their amazement, the very church and congregation to which, in his dream in Scotland he had preached, and which he so vividly described that they knew them at once. Verily God "led them in a way they knew not." The sequel showed still more, that it was the direct handiwork of God. For this church, where his ministry was greatly blessed, became his sure stay and support—helped to educate and supply his family with all necessaries, and thus enabled him to carry out, in a measure, what had always been his wish—giving his whole time to the ministry.

Thus he was enabled to go out into destitute parts as well as to the churches and congregations he had planted, to proclaim the gospel in its purity to a perishing people. Out through upper Richmond, in the Dockery neighborhood, or Cartlege's creek; down by Fayetteville on the Cape Fear, through Duplin, New Hanover, and the adjacent regions, he spread the good seed, opened out highways, and built high and strong the walls about Zion. Behold now the fruit of the labors of the then "wrestling Jacob," but the now "prevailing Israel." This whole region, destitute, ignorant, superstitious, disinclined to the support of the gospel, now feel the need of and gladly sustain such mighty men of God as Monroe, Dargan, Thomas, Beattie, the Culpepers, Lennon, Cobb, Alderman and Pittman, besides doing much for the spread of the gospel abroad. See, too, the refinement and general intelligence so apparent throughout all this section. They are pre-eminently an educated, religious and reading people.

Passsing once through Wadesboro, and a stranger there then, among a few in conversation, of whom he was one, the writer heard Judge Little remark of this Scotch community:

"I have seen many sections of our country, but do not know a region where education and refinement are more generally diffused than in lower Richmond and the adjacent parts."

Hon. Thos. S. Ashe, replying, said:

"That, too, has been my observation, and I think it leads the State in these respects."

Such remarks from such men plainly illustrate what a mighty work has been wrought in less than three quarters of a century; and in this, sound Bible truth, wielded by such earnest and loving men of God as Elder White, had much to do.

After making the Welch Neck church, S. C., the center of his operations for several years, he moved to Spring Hill, N. C., which had rapidly strengthened, and near here located his family permanently. He had serious trials and hardships to encounter in the commencement of his ministry in this section. Himself and wife were both earnest, zealous workers—she in the missionary societies, Sunday schools and prayer meeting, and he in the pulpit and "every good word and work"—yet they were but poorly paid, and their accommodations and support were often very poor. Once when Elder White was on a preaching tour from home, which was then a small rented log house, near Dr. Shaw's present residence, about a mile from the church, Mrs. White, leaving their child in the house, went to a spring some distance off for water. Here she saw a strange, large black animal which stood directly in her way, showing a disposition to attack. Affrighted, she ran to the house, where she met several men with guns—among them Arch'd Monroe, a brother of Elder Monroe—who told her they were in pursuit of a bear. She told them where she saw it, and they continued the chase; but the thought of such dangerous attendants as bears upon her isolated home made it very uncomfortable.

When their older children were large enough to watch

over the smaller, Mrs. White often accompanied her husband to his appointments. Once, while they were off some distance from home, a mighty tornado arose at night. The old people yet tell of the awful horrors of that night. Mrs. White was almost frantic with fear for her children, and with her husband hoped and prayed that they might be moved to go into a new strong kitchen they had built. "But," said the husband, "they are in the hands of God. He will guide them for the best," and threw off all apparent fear or concern. When they reached home they found the children had barricaded the doors and remained unhurt in the dwelling, while the *strong new kitchen*, outhouses, large trees, and piazza of the dwelling were blown down.

One of the secrets of Elder White's great usefulness and power was his perfect faith and trust in God.

CHAPTER VI.

SCOTCH BAPTISTS.

ANOTHER incident, illustrative of the love of his flock for him, may here be given. A Mr. Sanders, living near Society Hill, S. C., and who had enjoyed his ministry prior to his removal to Spring Hill, N. C., never failed, during the life time of Elder White, to come yearly to see him, though the distance was about fifty miles, bringing with him a barrel of flour and valuable cooper-ware each time, as presents to his father in Christ.

Spring Hill was not chosen by him as the place of his permanent residence on account of its superior congeniality to himself or family, but as a point where he believed he could accomplish the most good. Here he met with opposition on baptism under the water as the true mode; here he was poorly paid for his services, and here surrounded by a people wandering in the mazes of superstition—believing in witchcraft and ghosts—

> " Far out on the mountains wild and bare,
> Far away from the tender Shepherd's care."

But they were the people of his native land—his loved Scotland—thus going astray from the true fold, and this decided him.

Here, soon after his settlement, he one night preached a very able sermon against the superstitious beliefs of the people (a sermon said by the old people to be the most powerful they ever heard, and which uprooted their

ancient superstitions), and on returning to his home, with
head bowed in deep meditation, he suddenly lifted his
eyes and saw before him, in the pale moonlight, what appeared to be a tall figure in the white habiliments of the
grave, gently waving to and fro.   There it was directly
by the roadway before him ! . The cold sweat gathered upon
his brow at the fear that Heaven had sent it as a rebuke
for his temerity in speaking as he did.   If it be of God,
thought he, I will at least attempt to learn His will.   He
approached the object, and found it to be a bunch of tall
dog-fennel, white in the moonlight and frost!   Thus he
saw the optical illusion by which the startled believers in
the supernatural held to and spread their belief against
all reason.   From this time superstition, with its con-
comitant horse-shoes before doors and salt around dwell-
ings, disappeared from all the regions around Spring
Hill.

SCOTCH SERVICE,

or preaching and singing in the Gaelic language, was in-
dispensable for many years in the churches throughout
the Scotch region.   Many of the old Highlanders could
scarcely speak a word in the English language, and could
not at all follow a regular discourse in it.   To such Elder
White preached regularly in their native language; English in the morning and Gaelic in the evening was the
usual order.   Well does the writer remember the exceeding impressiveness of the Scotch service, as conducted in
later years.   In the evening, when the preacher entered
the church, the grave, stately and dignified old Scotchmen, with their attendant dames, would file slowly and

solemnly in. No people (bless their memory) reverenced God, His church and service more than they. We give the Scotch and English of a brief hymn:

SALM CXXXIII.

1. O feuch, cia meud am maith anis,
    cia meud an tlachd faraon,
    Braithrean, a bhi nan comhnuidh ghna
    an sith 's an ceangal caoin.

2. Mar ola phrifeil air a' cheann,
    ruidh air an fheufaig fios, ·
    'S s feufag Aroin, agus fhruth
    gu iomall eudaich 'ris.

3· Mar dhealt air Hermon, 's mar an druchd
    air fleibhtibh, Shioin fhus;
    'N fin dh'orduich Dia am beannuchadh,
    a bheatha fhiorruidh bhuan.

PSALM CXXXIII.

1. Behold, how good a thing it is,
    And how becoming well,
    Together, such as brethren are,
    In unity to dwell !

2. Like precious ointment on the head,
    That down the beard did flow,
    Ev'n Aaron's beard, and to the skirts
    Did of his garments go.

3. As Herman's dew, the dew that doth
    On Zion's hill's descend;
    For there the blessing God commands,
    Life that shall never end.

Which being given out, every one would enter with zest

into the singing. We always heard them sing to one tune—a common-metre—said to be Communion. The individual traits of each singer stood out in bold relief—some fast, some slow—but all indescribably solemn. The impressive prayer, and then the sermon. During the delivery of this, no beholder—no matter though utterly ignorant of the language—could well refrain from tears. There under the droppings of the sanctuary were the bowed gray heads, heedless of everything but the "words of life" to which they were listening; while

> "——Oft the big, unbidden tear,
>   Stealing down the furrowed cheek,
> Told, in eloquence sincere,
>   Tales of woe they could not speak."

Most of these noble old pioneers have gone to their reward—

> " Their mem'ry a blessing,
>   Their friendship a truth,"

and the world made better that they lived in it.

These, through the instrumentality of Elder White, were indeed led by a way that they knew not, and crooked things were made straight to them.

APPEARANCE AND TRAITS.

The Rev. Daniel White was of a pleasing and commanding appearance and address; well-built and broad-shouldered; of a thoughtful and gentle caste of countenance, black hair and eyes, and fair complexion. He greatly loved children, and always won their love. Of active, penetrating mind, and never at rest when not tively engaged in his Master's service, in which he was oquent, and urged the truth, in love, upon all he could ach. He was patient under hardships, and very little ncerned about worldly gains or losses. To illustrate: is three horses were one summer day in the pasture, hen there came up a sudden thunder-shower. A heavy ap of thunder, followed by the appearance of one of the orses, frightened and crippled, caused his wife to take er bonnet and shawl. "Where, wife?" said he. "To t the other horses," said she; "they might be struck ith lightning." "And if they are," said he, "you can-ot help them, and you must not endanger yourself." fter the shower his servant told him the two horses were illed. "Well," said he composedly, "bury them there." Vith him earthly things, in comparison with heavenly iings, were accounted as nothing; with him the salva-on of souls was the one thing needful. "Many souls for is hire" was his great and paramount aim. The value f one soul he estimated at more than ten thousand orlds like this. Therefore, soul prosperity—building igh and strong the walls of his beloved Zion, the spread f Christ's kingdom upon the earth—was his first, great nd almost only concern.

SEASONS OF REFRESHING.

His zeal and earnestness, as well as his willingness to o wherever he could accomplish the most good, caused im often to be sent to distant fields, to labor as mis-onary in Associational bounds. One year, while thus

engaged in the Raleigh Association, his labors were s
nally blessed at Louisburg, Franklin county, N. C. 1
services were held at an old-fashioned stand, surround
by arbors covered with green twigs and branches fr
the trees. The congregation was immense—many fr
Raleigh and a distance were there. It was described a
pentacostal season indeed. With the very beginning
the service, the Holy Spirit seemed to come down w
great power upon the congregation ; and before the clc
nearly the whole vast concourse were upon their kne
crying, earnestly, " What must we do to be saved ?" Ma
were converted and baptized during this meeting. Mu
good was done, and many blessings followed the labors
the Rev. Daniel White during this year in the Assoc
tion.

Some time about the year 1820, there was a genui
revival of religion at Spring Hill, the good fruits
which are till this very day apparent. During a qu&
terly meeting there, Elder White perceived manifestatio
of a work of grace in his congregation. He, therefore, (
Sunday appointed preaching at his own house. Oppo
tunely, on that night the Rev. Messrs. Dossey and Dani
(William Dossey, so well known as author of the " Choic
hymn book, and R. T. Daniel, Corresponding Secretary
the Home and Foreign Mission Board) stopped at Eld
White's, on their way from Fayetteville to Cheraw, S.
Thus reënforced by such able and zealous men of Go
Elder White made preparations and a goodly congreg&
tion assembled. Preaching began, and, said an eye-wi
ness, then a young girl, " there were old people and youn
men and maidens, right before me, crying aloud and cal

mercy. My heart was deeply touched, and I never
forget the scene." After the manner and zeal of Paul,
se faithful ministers continued preaching all night,
I in the morning there was great rejoicing in that
ase as well as in the Courts of Heaven over the "gather-
home" of poor prodigals—happy converts in their
liest love. Many of those who then joined, afterwards
ame pillars in the church, and all "did what they
ld for the Master."

Among others who joined at that meeting was Elder
hn Monroe. He was the only son of a devoted and
us mother, a zealous and faithful follower of her Sa-
ur. She was present, and we can easily imagine the
ng of prayer and praise that went up from her glad
art to the throne of mercy and love.

To show the earnestness for the salvation of souls per-
ding all ranks at this time, we may mention that a few
ys after this meeting, Elder White was plowing in his
ld. Mr. Leitch, a sturdy, pious farmer of the neighbor-
od, sternly—almost fiercely—bade him, in a loud voice
m the highway, "My brother, leave that plow! Drop
ur reins! Go out; tell sinners their danger—tell them
God, of heaven, of hell! Go, and God will bless you."
As Elder White's pilgrimage upon earth drew nearer
a close, his services were more signally blessed and
ned of God. He could look back upon the travail
his soul and be satisfied at the mercy and goodness of
e great Captain of his salvation.

Rev. John Monroe says of Elder White at this time:
In those early days, when the churches were few and
ak, he labored extensively as an evangelist. His efforts

were greatly blessed in Duplin and New Hanover cou
ties. Among the seals of the ministry in this region w
Elder George Fennell, in his day one of the most popul
and useful ministers in the Eastern Association.

We cannot forbear relating further of this able a
worthy divine that, when a young man and preparing
go the State Legislature to which he had been elect
Elder White stopped at his father's on Saturday night
have preaching at the neighboring church on Sunda
Young George Fennell, though not a professor of religio
said he could not attend church on the morrow, as he w
compelled to make preparations to go to the Legislatur
" My son," said his pious old father, " what is the State, t
nation, or the world compared to your soul's salvatio
tion. You may never hear another Gospel sermon, m
son. You must go to church." Young George Fenne
did go to church, and was on that day "convinced of si
of righteousness, and of an awful judgment to come," ar
became a true and happy convert, and afterwards a fait
ful minister of the gospel. Elder Fennell went and pe
formed his public duties well, but returned home full
imbued with the spirit that it is " better to be a doo
keeper in the house of the Lord than to dwell in the ten
of wickedness." He wrote a very affecting letter to Elde
White, styling him throughout as " Dear Father," an
urging him to come up to the " help of the Lord agains
the mighty;" to come over and help gather in the prodi
gal sons, of which there were so many in his region, t
their father's house. Thus we see how diligently Elde
White " sowed beside all waters," and how the rich fruit
were returning to him as his "crown of rejoicing." W

over what a wide field he set the armies of the living
d in array against the powers of darkness. He waved
;h the banner of the Cross; he buckled about them the
ole armor of the unerring Word. Amidst the darkest
rs and severest trials, his faith remained firm and un-
ken. Unmindful alike of man's censures or praises,
fought on for God and for Truth.

> " Faith, mighty faith, the promise sees,
>   And looks to that alone;
>   Laughs at impossibilities,
>   And cries, ' It shall be done' !"

And as his faith, so it was with him.

CHAPTER VII.

A Chapter of Incidents.

THERE are no truer sayings than that the " memory of
the just is blessed," and that a " good name is bett
than riches." Since the death of the Rev. Daniel Whi
many events have occurred, going to prove the greatne
of his life's work, and how deeply he has moved the pe
ple among whom it was his lot to labor.

But a few years ago, John Monroe Johnson, Esq., wa
travelling in a buggy, in South Carolina, seventy-fiv
miles from home, when, seeing a feeble old lady on th
highway, apparently tired out with walking, he aske
her to ride with him. As they rode on, she spoke of th
goodness and mercy of God, showing a deeply piou
nature and a heart at rest in her Saviour. Passing a ver
old church, she pointed her trembling finger to it, say
ing : " Oh, what times of refreshing—what peace—pa
understanding, God has given us there, under the preacl
ing of that mighty man of God, Rev. Daniel White
Mr. Johnson informed her that he was his grand-so
Whereupon the old lady put her arms about his neck an
wept upon his shoulder. She told him many of th
noble deeds and traits of his ancestor—his faith—h
power—his goodness—his purity of heart and life, cau
ing the grandson to feel the full force of the truth th
the " memory of the just is blessed."

Rev. E. L. Davis, of Anson, in a speech on missions before the Baptist State Convention in 1878, narrated with
thrilling effect, that he had *recently* baptized an old man,
who dated his conviction and subsequent conversion to
a sermon he heard the Rev. Daniel White preach in his
boyhood.   Not only in the times when his eloquent voice
was heard and his earnest manner beheld were these
seasons of refreshing enjoyed—for often then there were
pentecostal seasons "—but for half a century these burning words have been contending for the mastery over
natural indwelling sin, and finally triumphed!   Those
words of truth, like winged arrows showered among the
doves, have through all these years, kept them "flocking
to the windows," or like poor prodigals returning weak
and heart sore to their "father's house."   Oh the power
of true goodliness—the "foolishness" of preaching!

> Come, saith the living preacher—
> After death his voice echoes come !
> "Come," saith the Spirit !
> The Bride saith "come."
>
> "Come, saith Jesus' sacred voice,
> Come, and make my paths your choice,
> I will guide you to your home;
> Weary wanderer, hither come."

Though dead, the righteous "yet speaketh."   "Their
works do follow them."   Their good name and holy lives
tells the impenitent, "So prepare to meet thy God."

Their awakening words, long after their bodies have
crumbled to dust, still whisper warning and counsel to
the wayward :

> "Repent, O sinner, for you must die!"

Oh, how many are still preaching *here*, whose glorified spirits are singing praises to the Most High in the eternal courts above!

Who does not feel

> Jesus, lover of my soul,
> Let me to thy bosom fly."

Who does not desire to live the life of the righteous, that our last end may be like his? Jesus is the " way," the " door," the " life,"—and can make a

> —" Dying bed
> Feel soft as downy pillows are."

Once in the Ashpole section of Robeson county, as some there desired to hear him, Rev. Daniel White, as the Baptists had no church there, asked of another denomination the privilege of preaching in their church. All were willing but one elder. Elder White therefore, in deference to him, declined preaching in the church, but pointing to the groves he said, " the earth is the Lord's and the fullness thereof, therefore on His footstool we will serve Him." And there in the open grove, he delivered a very able discourse. Near this place a goodly Baptist brotherhood now assemble to worship, in a comfortable church called Mount Moriah. Though gentle and modest in his disposition, yet while about his Master's business, nothing could daunt or swerve him from the path of duty. If he had an appointment to preach,

he people well knew that only death or some similar
calamity could prevent its fulfillment. Storms, tempests,
loods or opposition, formed but feeble impediments to
him.

The quick gathering tempest of his native land, and
its fierce mountain torrents, surpassed anything here·
While in Scotland he had preached in the face of banishment or any punishment malice could invent. What,
therefore, cared he for the feeble opposition offered in a
land of liberty of conscience, when the salvation of his
people was concerned. Thus in many places he opened
out highways, fitted up springs in thirsty lands, cheered
the strong, assisted the weak, and administered consola-
to those " ready to faint."

Upon one occasion just before starting on one of his
long missionary tours, Elder White found that his family
were out of corn. Therefore he went for the needful sup-
plies, as the most likely place to get it at once, to a
wealthy but miserly and isolated neighbor, who he knew
had an abundance. This man knew he had no time to
look around for better terms, as his appointments were
out, therefore he took advantage of the situation, and
charged $2.00 a bushel for corn—almost double the then
ruling price. Elder White took it and when his family
complained of the extortion, he forbade them, saying they
" must not judge." Years afterwards, the great wealth
of this man, which he prized so much, was swept away,
and he came to the family of Elder White for corn—

which they let him have at a very low figure. Sinking
still lower in this world's goods, as well as infirmities,
they administered to his wants without remuneration.

This incident is introduced merely to show a trait in
the character of Elder White, which was never to complain—never to "judge," even though injustice or extortion were done him. It shows, too, how poor a bauble
wealth is—riches, often, very suddenly, "take to themselves wings and fly away."

——————

As an illustration of the remains of intolerance against
the Baptists, we may instance the case of Mr. Achibald
Graham, a most estimable man, who was engaged to be
married to a lady. The day for the marriage was set,
and all things made ready, when just before the happy
occasion his intended bride found that he inclined to immersion as the right mode of baptism. Not knowing
that in this desire of obedience to the Divine command,
he had committed an unpardonable offense, he repaired
at the appointed time to the home of his beloved, to claim
her as his bride. There the company was assembled, the
minister and waiters all present. All was ready but the
expectant bride—an important adjunct at such a cere-
mony. She could not be induced to come forward—for
she *would not* marry a Baptist! What then?

One of the brides-maids, a cousin of Mr. Graham, an
accomplished and beautiful lady, pittying, it may be, the
sad plight of her cousin, and pity is said to be akin to
love—stepped forward and offered to become his bride.

This offer he gladly accepted, and they were then and there made one. They were a happy couple, and he was a useful Deacon and exhorter in the Spring Hill church, over which Elder White was pastor.

Elder White was greatly pleased when Spring Hill church was organized, as he well might have been, from the material of which it was composed. They were his countrymen. They were strong in the faith, and in a community where Baptists before that time were little known. They were nearly all his children in Christ. Mr. John White, a nephew of his, saw a letter he was writing to his friends in Scotland about this joyful event, in which he well remembers the passage: "I have organized a church at Spring Hill, North Carolina, consisting of seven members, all of whom except my wife, are my children in Christ." No doubt the whole letter was full of love and praise to God.

CHAPTER VIII.

His Work for Missions.

Most of our readers have doubtless made themselves familiar with the lives and labors of those great and good men, Adoniram Judson and Luther Rice. They know of their having been sent by opposers of baptism by immersion as missionaries to Burmah. They know that out in mid ocean their Bibles and prayers for God's guidance, without any human influence, brought them into the Baptist faith and belief. Therefore, cut off from the denomination by which they were sent out, they had to seek aid from the Baptists, that they might seek the salvation of those benighted heathen. They know of Luther Rice's return for this purpose, of his success in his efforts, and of his mighty work for the Columbian College. They know, too, that the Baptists did sustain Judson and other faithful missionaries abroad. They know how signally God has blessed those mighty missionaries, as instruments in His hands for the conversion of the heathen. But they may not know of the ceaseless and tireless labors of Elder White and his zealous and energetic wife in this direction. The Rev. Luther Rice often made the home of Elder White his abiding place in his missionary tours through the country, and in him and his family he found congenial spirits in his noble efforts for the spread of the gospel in heathen lands. Elder White's labors in this direction were indeed herculean ; and so great was the impetus by which his eloquence and

example imbued the Baptists throughout the whole broad
belt in which he preached, that they have abated but little till this day, and such a name as "Hardshell" we do
not think exists in it.   Nor was his wife any less zealous
in her humbler sphere.   She inaugurated a Woman's
Missionary Society, all being required to make systematic
contributions for Foreign Missions.   They secured funds
mostly by the sale of chickens, eggs, butter and such like
articles as they could sell at McLeod's Hotel, on the stage
road between Fayetteville, N. C., and Cheraw, S. C.   They
even believed that these things increased on their hands
in the ratio of their sales, and that they still had as many
chickens, &c., after all their sales and contributions to
missions, as did those who did not sell or contribute anything.   We can readily believe it for the widow's flour
was something like that.   Mrs. White also enlisted the
young people—boys and girls of the neighborhood—to do
what they could for the poor heathen.   The children in
the Children's Missionary Society were to contribute ten
cents quarterly for this object.

Both of these societies, under the guidance of Mrs.
White, were successfully conducted, and contributed much
to the aid of Foreign Missions.   To show the alacrity with
which the children entered into the work, we may instance the case of a poor family, by the name of Watson,
in their neighborhood.   Mrs. Watson—an earnest, zealous Baptist and faithful worker—taugh her children in
the way they should go ; and Hugh, her son, a member
of the society, took great pleasure in contributing when
he could get the means.   One day, almost desponding of
securing his quarterly mite, he brought, as a present, a

few fish he had caught to Mrs. White. She gave him a
shilling, "and," said she, "he leaped about like David
before the Ark, with joy, exclaiming, 'O, I can give this
to the poor heathen.'" This Mr. Hugh Watson was
afterwards a pillar in the church, and was greatly pros-
pered in his home, near Selma, Alabama, where he took
his mother and the family. Afterwards, on a visit to
his native State and to Mrs. White, he informed her that
from that early age he had resolved to give as the Lord
increased him, and he was then giving fifty dollars yearly
to the cause.

The writer well remembers his manly figure, benign
countenance and touching address, as, on one of his visits
to North Carolina, Rev. John Monroe asked him, after
service on the Sabbath, if he would not say something.
He arose, and in melting language portrayed the joys of
Christian fellowship and reunion, quoting a verse of
Burns:

> " It heats me, it beats me,
> It sets me on flame,
> It warms me, it charms me," &c.,

to be in His church and among His people. The name
of Jesus is sweet, is precious here, but how glorious it will
be to be with Him and His redeemed in heaven! "Oh,"
said he, "I had rather be a doorkeeper in the house of the
Lord than dwell in the tents of wickedness."

Such were the children reared under the teaching of
Elder White and his wife, and in the true nurture and
admonition of the Lord.

Besides the Missionaries Socities, Mrs. White organized
a Wednesday night meeting, held in rotation at the

houses of the members of the church. These meetings were continued through a period of about forty years, and they were the means of introducing the gospel, in its purity, to many in the neighborhood of members who, but for this means, would have been almost without it. In these meetings, too, the members did not neglect the assembling of themselves often together, and the good fruits were seen and felt through that long period.

ELDER WHITE'S LAST JOURNEY.

For some days before he started on his last missionary tour, Elder White, although apparently in his usual good health, expressed his belief that his work on earth was nearly finished, and manifested unusual anxiety for putting " his house in order," and in arranging for the well-being and future comfort of his family. He advised his wife of his premonitions, and asked her to accompany him. She urged the press of business in preparations for an Association at Welch Neck, South Carolina, which he was to attend immediately on his return from Duplin and New Hanover counties, and to which she and other members of the family would accompany him. After bidding his family farewell and going to the gate, where his horse awaited him, he returned to the house to ask his wife if she could not accompany him. She replied that, though she wished much to do so, she could not. He then bade all an affecting, and what proved to be a last farewell upon earth.

Elder White went out through Fayetteville and down the Cape Fear to his field of labor in the Cape Fear Asso-

ciation. He engaged in earnest preaching, and in the
midst of one of his sermons he was stricken down by sickness. He was removed by gentle and loving hands to
the house of Mr. Henry, where, after two days of fever,
which they did not consider dangerous, he suddenly grew
worse and died, in the full assurance of a blissful immor-
tality.

Here ended the earthly life of this great and good man
of God, in the year 1824.

In the mean time his wife had heard nothing of his
sickness or death. The preparations for the Associational
trip were completed. The family were all in the eager
anticipation that night of the return of the loved husband and father. In the evening, Mrs. White called upon
a sick neighbor, intending to be back home in time to
meet her husband. That evening Mrs. Gilchrist received
a letter for Mrs. White with the black seal, indicative of
death. Opining its sad import, and believing no one
could so gently break the news as herself to her friend,
she took the letter and found Mrs. White at the sick
neighbor's. As Mrs. White prepared to leave, Mrs. Gilchrist accompanied her, and when some distance on the
way, she handed her the letter. Mrs. White read, and
dropping the letter, fell helpless into the arms of her
friend. Mrs. Gilchrist soothed her as best she could, and
then accompanied her home, evincing a degree of sensi-
tive refinement which only true hearts contain. Another
shock to the bereaved family was the return of the horse
and empty saddle. Now they felt all the bitterness and
pain of their mighty loss, but consolation came in the
knowledge that he had battled bravely and fallen glori-

ously in the service of the Great King, to whom he had committed them, and with whom he was now gone to live forever and ever.

Elder White's concern for his family before his last journey was not unnoted by Him who numbers the hairs of the head and bottles up the tears of his saints, as well as "tempers the winds to the shorn lamb," notices every sparrow that falls to the ground, and hears the young ravens when they cry for food. Every member of his family were early gathered into the fold and nurtured under "the tender Shepherd's care." His family, too, were abundantly blest in "basket and in store," and how sweet and

> ——" precious was the gift
> He to his loved ones gave—
> The stainless memory of the just,
> The wealth beyond the grave."

Some years afterwards, Mrs. White and her son-in-law, Charles Livingston, placed a tomb-stone over the dust of this noble man of God, and did all that loving hearts could to decorate his last resting place. Here, then, where his peaceful body will rest till the last trump will summon all nations to the judgment, is it not well we should ask "What think ye of Christ?"

Elder White thought Him "the chief among ten thousand, and the one altogether lovely." In Him he trusted, for Him he labored, and for that labor of love he forsook home, country, friends, and all his heart esteemed so dear, and in Him yielded up his spirit, in the blissful assurance of a glorious eternity. Over death and the grave he could cry out in the triumphs of victory: "I know that my Redeemer liveth."

How awful, in comparison, the death scenes of Voltaire, Paine and the wretched infidels who went shrieking away, without "God or hope in the world." How with poor Queen " Bess," who lived only for glory? "My kingdom for an inch of time." With Lord Chesterfield, who lived only for self and formal vanities? In substance, he exclaimed: "I have estimated life at its full value; I have counted the cost; and though I have *no hope* in the future, yet I would not live over life again." With Lord Byron, who only lived for fame and vanity?

> " My life is in the sere and yellow leaf,
>   Love's pleasures gone—
> For me the canker and the grief
>   Remain alone !"

With Paul, who lived for Christ? "I have fought a good fight, I have kept the faith, I have finished the work Thou gavest me to do. Henceforth there is laid up for me a crown of righteousness, which God, the righteous Judge, will give me in that day." Thus die the believers and those who believe not in Jesus.

> " The battle of our life is brief :
>   The alarm, the struggle, the relief,
> Then sleep we side by side."

Jesus, in the depth of his love for our fallen race, cried out in his last agonies: "Father, forgive them, for they know not what they do." From the high courts of heaven He came down to suffer poverty that we might be rich ; and, oh, wondrous love ! while we were yet enemies, He died that we might live.

Though the Ingersolls, Darwins, Huxleys and Tyndalls may raise their feeble arms against Him, let it be ours to cleave the closer to Him—to attempt each day to love Him more and serve Him better. He is our Saviour—the way and the life—the door to heaven. With Him, we have a right to the tree of life—to go in through the gates into the city. Without Him, we are lost with all the nations who forget God. He loved us. He died for us:

> " Only Jesus, only Jesus,
> Can do helpless sinners good."

Like Elder White--like the good and true men through all the ages—let us attempt to be faithful servants in His vineyard; and in word, thought and deed, do all we can for the Master, that at last, with the glorious throng at His right hand, we may hear the welcome plaudit, " Well done, ye blessed of my Father."

CONCLUSION.

We have given, dear reader, a brief and imperfect sketch of a great and useful life, the contemplation of which can only tend to good. Elder White was about 40 years old at his death, and his bereaved widow survived him forty-two years, devoting that time to the furtherance of her Redeemer's kingdom; and at her death, which occurred on January 29th, 1867, it was found that she had (out of the wreck left her by Sherman's army) bequeathed $50 to Foreign Missions, $50 to Wake Forest College, and $100 to her beloved pastor, Elder Monroe.

Of her, how truly it may be said :

> " Thy soul, renewed by grace divine,
>   In God's own image, freed from clay,
> In heaven's eternal sphere shall shine
>   A star of day."

MRS. CATHERINE WHITE.

EVENTS IN SCOTLAND.

A FEW incidents and events may here be given, in illustration of the great awakening and manner of preaching in Scotland about the years 1799 and 1800.

A rumor was heard from a distance in the Highlands, of a mighty preacher turning things upside down by the power of his ministry. Some said he was mad—and those who heard him partook of his malady. Some said he was of God—because his preaching was like that of John the Bapt st in the wilderness of Judea. Others held that he must be possessed of a devil—from the power he had over assemblies, and from the authorities not taking and banishing him though he had been heard of in several quarters. Others again, believed that his work must be pure and good—because it was said men notoriously wicked had been changed about to excellent men after they had heard him. Thus conjecture, surmise, wonder and doubt were abroad in the land—and many, led by curiosity and other causes, managed to hear him. Very many of those who went with light and frivolous views, returned after they had heard him under a mighty burthen of unpardoned sin—with the keen arrows of conviction impelling them to cry for mercy. Among others, Duncan and Effie Campbell, brother and sister of Catharine Campbell, (afterwards Mrs. White), were at a distance from their home in Rosneth, and heard him and were both brought to a saving knowledge of the truth. They returned home, "renewed in the spirit of their minds," greatly to the mortification of Catherine and her gay, dancing school companions.

Effie and Duncan took no delight in balls and dancing parties now. Catherine and her companions, or dancing school mates, determined they would make Effie attend a ball, which was at a neighbor's house, beyond a pool of water. For this purpose they watched their opportunity, they surrounded her and took her by main strength, despite her efforts to the contrary, until they reached the pool of water, where, being attracted by the thickness of the ice, they left their prisoner, for the moment, and went to skating upon it. While they were absorbed in this amusement, Effie slipped away, and they had to go to the ball without her.

A few weeks after this, Catherine was thrown into consternation, by learning that her brother Duncan had invited the great McArthur, who had stirred up Scotland, to preach at their house on a certain night. She first determined she would attend dancing school that night—but was over-persuaded to remain and hear him—much as she disliked to. He came, and she took her position in a corner behind him, to see and hear, but not be seen, "but," said she, "he saw me and all the company in that sermon, and all were won by him—he was so sincere, strong and true—and several were brought under deep convic-tion." A Mr. Lamont was at their house that night, and a few days afterwards she heard that he had been

BORN AGAIN,

and Mr. McArthur would preach at his house the next night. Amazed beyond measure (for she was not a Bible reader,) she determined she would go—the man after the change of such a marvellous nature being the main ob-ject of her curiosity. The only change that she saw was that Lamont looked happy and at rest, whereas he had always before been wild and boisterous!

The next appointment was at an old ruin, near by, where, as it was to be in the day time, she and her dan-cing companions concluded to get on the old crumbling wall, that formed part of the enclosure and have rare fun all to themselves. "But," said she, "I could think of nothing but the sermon—the burning words of truth and soberness—and before it was over, I was fain to hide my-self under the shadow of the wall, and weep and cry for mercy upon my sin-burthened soul."

Rev. John Monroe says:

"Through the instrumentality of Daniel McArthur, a faithful and zealous young minister, God was pleased graciously to revive His work in Scotland about the year 1800. Many were drawn from a distance, together, by the reports of the good work which spread rapidly through the country. Among those who came through mere curiosity, was Mrs. White, who was soon made to feel the quickening of the Holy Spirit; and after a season of pungent conviction, and unfeigned repentance, she was enabled to believe in the Lord Jesus Christ, and to rejoice in Him with joy unspeakable and full of glory."

The revival was great and wide spread; the preaching of a high order, and awakening in its pathos and power. God gave an abundant increase. We can plainly see, too, how in His wisdom, He *was* bringing from darkness into light a strong, influential, self-reliant nature—full of energy, zeal and power, for the arduous and trying hardships and responsible duties of the missionary life before her.

All who knew her know how well and faithfully she performed her part in the great work here in America. They know with what zeal and energy, after the death of her husband, she kept up meetings, missionary societies, family prayer-meetings; riding out long distances, holding prayer and religious conversations in families—endearing herself to old and young alike. Even little children would run to meet her—to tell her of their pet schemes; their play-houses; their birds and squirrels— as the writer well remembers doing in his early boyhood—in all of which she took a lively interest; won the young hearts and then pointed them to God, in His beauty, greatness and love—to Jesus, his precious Son, "the way and the Life," who died that sinful man might live. Through a very wide circle her influence for good was seen and felt, alike by young and old. With her the song of the redeemed was always welling up:

" 1. Canaibh do'n Tighearn' oran nuadh,
    gach aon tir, canaibh dha.

 2. Seinnibh do Dhia : ainm beannuichibh
    nochdaibh a shlaint' gach la.

3. Am meafg nam fineach aineolach
   sior thaisbeinnibh a ghloir :
Am measg nam poibleach innisibh
   a mhiorbhuile ro-mhor.

[TRANSLATION.]

1 O, sing a new song to the Lord—
   Sing all the earth to God.

2. To God sing, bless his name, shew still
   His saving health abroad

3. Among the heathen nations
   His glory do declare,
And unto all the people show
   His works that wondrous are."

Beside her great life-work in America, who can esti-
mate the good of her example and teaching to her companions and associates after her conversion in Scotland.
There, as here, her influence was great. Before conversion, she was the leader in gaiety. She was the pettied
child of her family. Bouyant and fun-loving in her
tastes, lively and animated to an unusual degree, she could
ill brook restraint. The Light shone in upon her dark-
ened mind, and she was changed. Her companions saw
the marvelous change; they heard her melting words of
love to God, and saw her earnest desire for their salvation
and the salvation of all. As the saints first distrusted the
converted Paul, from their remembrance of the persecut-

ing Saul of Tarsus, so must her companions have first distrusted her, till they saw that her whole mind, life and strength was devoted to good, righteousness, truth—to Jesus and His love. Then they felt that there was a reality and a mighty power in the religion she professed.

Mrs. White was a strong support to her husband in his great work. She left a hallowed memory of a well-spent life. She was always willing and ready to be about her Master's work. She sought in everything His name's glory and the advancement of His Kingdom, and she was ready at last, when the bridegroom came, with oil enough, and her lamp trimmed and burning. Now in Heaven—the beautiful Zion of her love—she is forever at Home.